To my family... Drink your milk! — A. S.

For Augurius, Alfonsus, Clementine, and Ambrose. — Mama (E. A.)

Text copyright © 2025 by Abbe Starr.
Illustration copyright © 2025 by Evelline Andrya.

All rights reserved. No part of this book may be reproduced in any manner or transmitted in any form without the express written consent of the publisher, except in the case of brief excerpts in critical reviews and articles.
For permission inquiries, please contact info@gnomeroadpublishing.com.

GNOME ROAD PUBLISHING
Louisville, Kentucky, USA
www.gnomeroadpublishing.com
Logo designs by Wendy Leach, copyright © 2025 by Gnome Road Publishing
Book design by Bonnie Kelso.

Summary: A unique look at the world's many different kinds of milk, from cow milk to coconut milk to oat milk and more.

ISBN: 978-1-957655-51-2 (trade) | ISBN: 978-1-957655-52-9 (ebook)

Library of Congress Control Number: 2024951434
LC record available at: https://lccn.loc.gov/2024951434
Illustrations were rendered with a combination of traditional and digital collage.
The text of this book is set in Merriweather and Eds Market fonts.

First Edition
10 9 8 7 6 5 4 3 2 1
Manufactured in China

Ahhh, Milk!

The Many Ways Milk Is Made

Written by
Abbe Starr

Illustrated by
Evelline Andrya

Like a stream gives and grows, on this earth, sweet milk flows.

In vast deserts,

by calm seas,

tundra,

tropics,

pastures,

trees.

Press then squeeze.
Squirt a spurt.

Heat,
strain,
pour . . .
rich dessert.

Ahhh, Milk!

In green meadows,

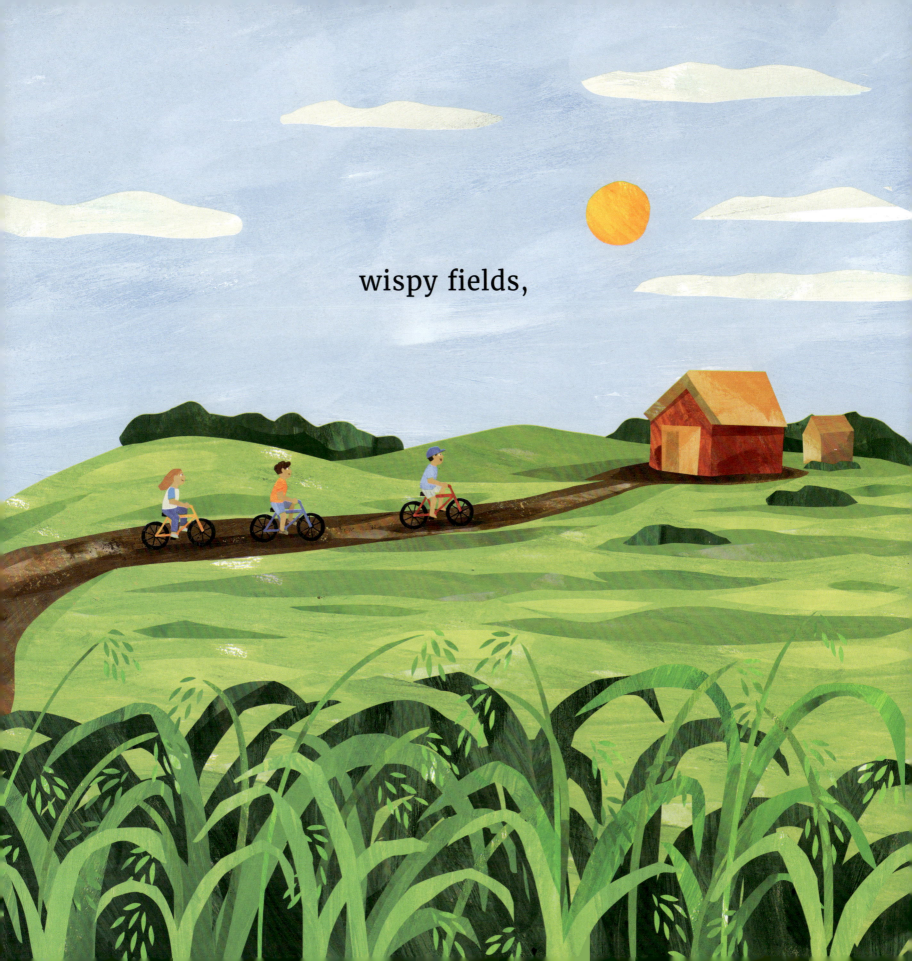

harvest yields.

Beans that bloom,

oats that sway,

take away.

Chop and stack.
Strip and thresh.

Sort,
soak,
blend.
Rest . . . refresh.

Ahhh, Milk!

In wild jungles,

or straight rows,

on warm shores
a seedling grows.

Cashews twist.
Almonds shake.

Coconuts . . .
crack and break.

Split and spread.

Pry, peel, stack.

Almonds:
Farmers shake almond trees to harvest their almonds.

Oats:
Oats are a heart-healthy ingredient for dairy-free milk.

Rice:
Rice milk is naturally gluten free.

Soybeans:
Soybeans produce milk low in calories and packed with protein.

Cashews:
Cashews grow from the bottom of their stems, which look like swollen pieces of fruit.

Coconuts:
Grated coconut meat is used to make a creamy milk popular in many countries around the world.

Reindeer:
Reindeer milk has more fat and protein than cow milk.

Camel:
Camel milk has less sugar than cow milk and is loaded with vitamins and minerals.

Cows:
Cow milk is known to help keep bones strong and healthy.

Water Buffalo:
Some Mozzarella cheese, paneer, yoghurt and ghee are made from water buffalo milk.

Donkey:
Donkey milk is reported to benefit the immune system and help hydrate skin.

Moose:
Moose milk is said to be good for the gut (your stomach). Moose cheese is one of the most expensive in the world.

About the Author:
Abbe grew up in the rolling hills of Wisconsin surrounded by fields and farms, *moos* and milk. She writes poetry, ready-to-read, and picture books. She is the author of several educational books and a storyteller in her home community, Ft. Wayne, Indiana. Abbe's favorite milk is coconut milk especially when it comes with a warm chocolate chip cookie! Visit: *abbelstarr.com* to learn more.

About the Illustrator:
Evelline was born in Sumatra, Indonesia and grew up with a mix of Chinese and Javanese cultures. She was influenced by vintage greeting cards that she found in her grandma's drawer, comic books, vintage picture books, and animated movies. She graduated from an academy of art and design in 2006 and started her freelance career in 2010. Since then, Evelline has illustrated more than 35 children's books. Her illustration style is a mix of traditional medium and digital collage. In her spare time, Evelline loves to create paintings with acrylics and watching behind the scenes of stop motion animated movies.

Visit our website to download our free educational guides and bonus materials. At Gnome Road, we want to provide you with materials to incorporate our books into your learning environments, depending on the needs of your classrooms or library centers.

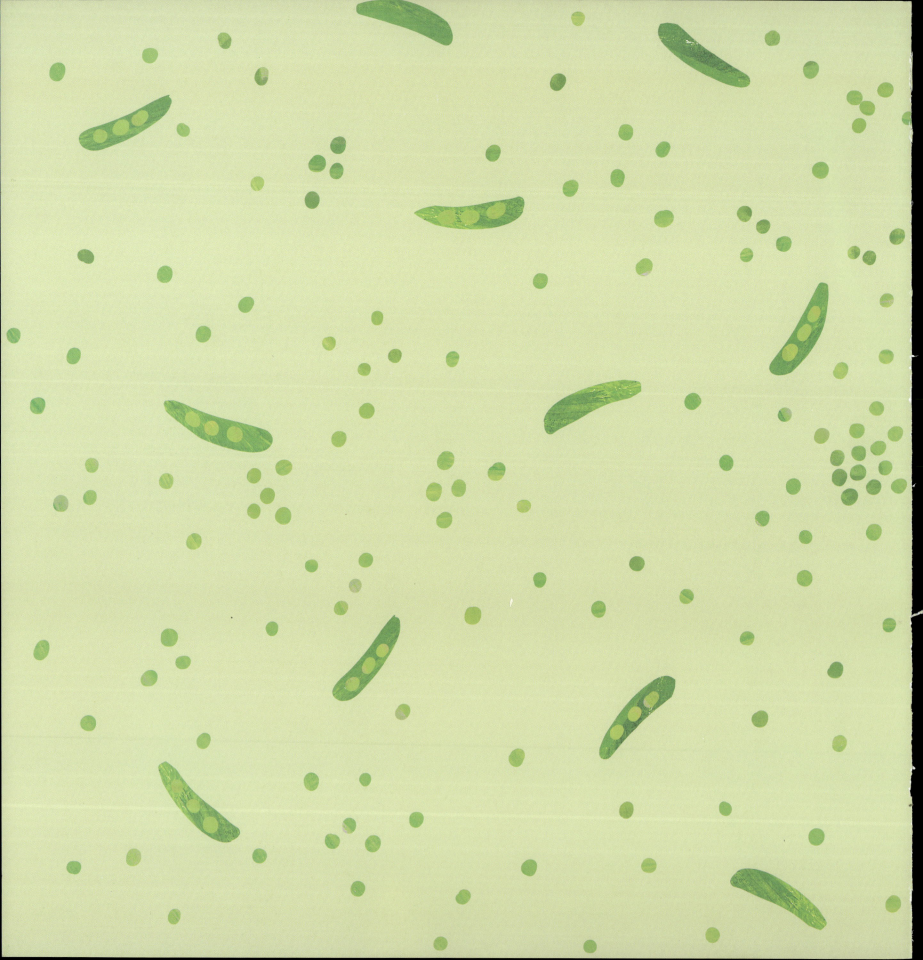